VERSES OF HEART, SOUL AND BLOOD

SHIRLEY SIATON

ALL MY PIECES
VERSES OF HEART, SOUL AND BLOOD

Copyright © 2024 Shirley Siaton Parabia

ALL RIGHTS RESERVED.
No part of this book may be reproduced or used in any manner without the prior written permission of the copyright owner, except for the use of brief quotations in a book review.

To request permission,
contact the publisher at books@inkysword.com.

ISBN 978-621-490-098-5 (pbk)

Published by Shirley S. Parabia
Cover design by Temptation Creations
Interior formatting by Mhy San Miguel

First Edition, March 2024

Inky Sword Book Publishing
Barangay Quezon, Arevalo, Iloilo City 5000
Republic of the Philippines
inkysword.com

To Peter, Arya & Selene

ALL MY PIECES

VERSES OF HEART, SOUL AND BLOOD

CONTENTS

The Collection

Part One: Shards of MyHeart
15 | Bitten
17 | Cradled Head
19 | Drought
21 | Drunk
23 | Dumbstruck
25 | Faceless
27 | First Taste
29 | Graduation Day
31 | Hidden
33 | Hungry
35 | Lavender Polish
37 | Living
39 | Long-Lost Tango
41 | Lover
43 | My Death Man
45 | Other
47 | Pimple
49 | Purple Scrunchie
51 | Regression
53 | Smoke
55 | Solstice
57 | Ugly

59 | Ulcer
61 | Wallflower
63 | Yellow-Green

Part Two: Wisps of My Soul
67 | Afar
69 | Arms
71 | Away
73 | Begging Streets
75 | Blue
77 | Damnation
79 | Danger
81 | Debt
83 | Deception
85 | Delusion
87 | Demolition
89 | Deprivation
91 | Despair
93 | Difference
95 | Disease
97 | Distance
99 | Disintegration
101 | Divination
103 | Duplication
105 | Dust
107 | Dwelling
109 | Fallen Frame
111 | Food Court
113 | Juxtaposition
115 | Rainfall

117 | Scars in Solitude
119 | The Voyage
121 | Untold

Part Three: Drops of My Blood
125 | A Fat Girl Thing
127 | Aimless
129 | Anchor
131 | Ardor
133 | Back in the Food Court
135 | Black Cat
137 | Blood
139 | Dark
141 | Dauntless
143 | Dawn
145 | Death
147 | Defiance
149 | Deliverance
151 | Depths
153 | Desire
155 | Destination
157 | Discord
159 | Disruption
161 | Divergence
163 | Divide
165 | Dreams
167 | Dribble
169 | Drift
171 | Flight
173 | Holy War

175 | Silence
177 | Smoke

THE COLLECTION

As with any good story, there were stages in my journey as a poet: the starting point, the exploration, and the endgame.

The initial stage was when I looked around me in wonder. I took on the role of chronicler, more witness than partaker, as events unfolded before my eyes.

In my earliest work, my poetry was inspired by random things and occurrences both captivating and mundane. This was a time when words flowed organically from my headspace, fearlessly diffusing ideas into the greater, wider world.

The middle of the excursion was quite the odyssey, a time to move and find my place under the sun.

I wrote all about the world I lived in; shared tales as witness to greed, destitution and despair. I shared unfettered views of unforgiving places and their dark corners.

My endgame, I would like to say, has always been to triumph over the adversities and trials of life.

This was far from the conclusion of my journey, but, instead, the pinnacle of what I believe poetry could achieve: capture one's tragedies and victories, hopes and dreams, loves and losses; share the sublime beauty of life, both in the shadows and in the light.

Many years after I typed down my first poem, I still marvel at how words could capture and immortalize the indefatigable hope in the human spirit, the very thing that fuels faith, ambition, and determination.

I have seen hope thrive in the darkest, most decrepit of places. I have witnessed remarkable feats of resilience and survival, pain morphing into impenetrable armor, and loss bringing forth new beginnings.

All My Pieces is a collection of poetry written across decades of my existence. Each poem in this book is a treatise from my heart, soul and blood; each verse is an honest testament to a life rife with beautiful intricacies, tribulations and triumphs.

This is a story of change, of someone who has grown with each drop of blood, sweat, and tears shed; of a woman who captured her voyage farther and further into the world in words.

And she has only just begun.

SHARDS OF MY HEART

*Bitten now and bleeding:
there's nothing in those sterile shelves
to ease my pain;
I just need you not to pour salt
into my gaping heart.*

BITTEN

I've been scratched and stabbed,
wounded to the point
of losing blood.
But I've never been hurt
the way I had
when I was bitten
by the bug.

Bitten now and bleeding:
there's nothing in those sterile shelves
to ease my pain;
I just need you
not to pour salt
into my gaping heart.

ALL MY PIECES | 17
VERSES OF HEART, SOUL & BLOOD

CRADLED HEAD

Now I try to say
sorry
and there's this stopper
up my larynx.
Unspoken remains
my regret.

There is the first
bitter whiff of bloom
thrown into the welcoming cradle;
the first gentle stab
into my weakling's fingers-
that thorn's vengeance.

I felt the ire
in its half-wilted petals.
Felt the blood
dry a deep red;
the pain a dull
thrumming in waxy ears.
Nothing more
but wind, smells,
and gooseflesh.

Longing for that resented
touch on my migraine-inhabited
head.
The throbbing flesh mixes
with the dewy earth.

DROUGHT

Yesterday
there was rain
in torrents
tearing away what is
and in hesitant streams
trickling as tears would.

Now
dried
and fraught with madness
rain is no more
and long gone.
Puddles pool
as final remembrance
slipping away
in the midday
heat.

DRUNK

Spun me around
in circles;
I took much
out of nothing
that was already there.

An emptiness
once filled to the brim
with everything
that mattered.

A wholeness
I swore
would never break.

Then again,
you came
and shattered it all
and made me
seek what I am.

DUMBSTRUCK

Now is not the time
To tell me that you're sorry
Just go on and don't look back
That's what I expect you to do

There is so much to say
Too many words rooted
In the depths of your eyes
You just can't put them to words

I've never said much, have I?
I'm mute as a mime when I'm near you
Then again, there's not much to say
For now, you're on your way

Don't say a word
Don't even look my way
Don't dare say you're sorry
Though I doubt I'll make it through another day
Without you
I have not said I love you
And now I've lost the chance to

Say goodbye
Allow me one final embrace
That I will feel
Forever.

FACELESS

Images of you
flicker
as candle-flames do
in a sultry night.

(Beckoning.)

Your voice
ripples
as molten gold does
in the North Wind's fleeting embrace.

I curse
the wrinkled paper
on which I draw
the eyes that had never laid on me.
I hate
the leaky pen
that sputters an endearment
or two
you may never even hear.

I wish
you were the remote control
I hold close
until sign-off.
That way,
there would be no more
goodbye.

FIRST TASTE

Pounding.

The weary floor resonates:
infectious with life and sound,
with strobes of varicolored light.
In flashes.
As fast as the young heart
pumps life,
as sharp as the senses
take in the reek of body heat.

My bareness
is shaped by your hands;
I move to the rhythm
shared by lone strangers
amidst the frenzy.
I forget the bitch wind
of night.

This is but the first touch.

As the swirling
gathers me into its billows,
I hold on to flesh, bone,
the unmasked scent of soap
and the unmistakable froth of anger
bubbling from burnished lips
and distinctly hear

The pounding.

GRADUATION DAY

It dawns like a day
Of impending doom:
I stand on the cracked second-floor corridor
And stare at the rusty bars
Of the three-decade-old balcony.

A guttural prayer escapes
my chapped lips
For I forgot the balm
(forgot to shoplift)
So I bite my dry lower lip
In supplication to a higher power.

My uniform is worn down,
The collar is blackish-brown;
Mama forgot to wash it (again):
The mahjong table takes up
Her laundry hours.

A footfall draws me to reality.
It was him:
A lanky boy of burnt-red skin
And a voice that sometimes squeaks
When he shouts to be fed
During basketball.

Dressed in scuffed brown-leather shoes
And a half-open shirtjack,
He reeks of a citrusy scent
That costs sixty-five pesos
A bottle.

He stops by my monobloc
And asks if he could copy our last assignment:
Ten multi-colored graphs in Calculus;
I say no
(I don't know why).

He shrugs and, whistling, walks away
Like everybody had in my
Four years spent in a
Tomb of things
I'd want to forget.

(And so
The toga tassel is turned
From back-left
to front right)

Yet will always remember.

HIDDEN

I never knew you,
I never even looked at you—
but there you were
a shadow among shadows.
If only I took the time
to see.

I heard you then:
a loud drumbeat after the next,
pounding to the steady rhythm
of a heart
long since watching
and waiting.

Now, I watch the unyielding downpour
wash away time
in runny puddles.
Now, I listen to the clock
ticking away,
taunting.

And I wait
for the moment—
that killing blow
when you turn
and walk away.

HUNGRY

The sustenance has gone stale,
and I don't want to swallow
perforated hopes that ride
the stillness and the emptiness
as I gaze at you.

Maybe you remind me
that I want to put something
in the void that throbs to be filled
so it can live-
and I think
I no longer want to.

I try so hard
to go down the pipes
like dishwater
when I want to drink you in
as my breath:
I still need to.

LAVENDER POLISH

i.   drizzles of laundry water
strip the shade
I had blended
from fleeting dreams;
leaving bare unlovely,
uneven surfaces
no one would look at
(not even me)

ii.   I scrub
the roughness
with a cotton ball
drenched in fortified-protein
hopes,
and I cringe;
the lavender fades
as would the bruises
from a post-Happy Hour
tantrum
he had thrown
countless times before:

iii.   now, I shake
the bottle
vigorously
just so I could

      paint the frosted purplish hue
      on my nails
      to color-coordinate

iv. I wait
     for the lavender
     to set
     to reappear
     on my flesh

LIVING

I live this strange little
existence—I don't even know
what it's supposed to be.
Strangled, laden with
shattered stuff:
fragments of a heart once beating
and pumping tangy blood.

I breathe this so-called air of life
that kills me with each
proverbial toke—
when I would have wanted the
glamor of cigarette smoke.

I roam the cruel streets
that scream of my
generation's apathy.
And bleed with red and sunny-yellow
and acetylene-white.
Words, their wisdom
long lost.

I love this wisp
of a being ready
to be snapped in two.
He's the one who
means so much;
enough that I just have to
go on.
Living.

LONG-LOST TANGO

How Time went past
driving ever southward
like sunbeams
welcoming dusk.

Songs long forgotten
lose what little melody
floating about in dreams—
too worn
from a quest
of finding fragments
once belonging
to you and me.

As the unknown dawns
once more: if we could dance
and know no fear
to the beat
of the long-lost tango.

Even if
scratchy phonographs
play silent music alone.

LOVER

When do you look?

There's nothing more
to life
but net and lines.

Of service overs and smashes;
squeaking and worn rubber shoes
against the cold concrete court
against the dreamscape.

This is a game of you, for you.

Forgetting and remembering
in glances
as fast as you move.

There is blood
beneath the sweat.

When do you see?

MY DEATH MAN

lightning strikes you
and you stand ramrod
straight
silver bullets pounce
on your obsidian heart
and you stand
impervious

what's your name,
my death man?
who are you
to take my breath
away
and leave me
seeking?
my death man,
come to me
relieve me of misery

the acid shower
caresses
your unyielding face
that I yearn to caress—
the downpour is reduced
to the trickles

of music
from your splintered guitar

daggers of desolation
draw your black-red blood
and my lips savor
its metal tang
then I drink
of your madness
and the coldness
of your love

my death man,
your music is my eternal lullaby
my death man,
your music is my elegy

OTHER

I was the one
Who looked at you from way
across the room
The one who felt your pain
And never gave it back
I cared not
If you can't even see
Just in dreams
Be with me

I was the girl
Who felt your touch
On her flesh
That gentleness from someone so strong
I cried not
If you love her
Just go on
Walking past

I was the other
You looked right through
I was part of you
That shudder in the hall
That whisper into the moonless sky
That gaze on your back as you walk towards her
That one
Loving you

PIMPLE

Just like a pimple:
You throbbed in my waking hours
taking time
as I tried
to scratch at you.

Just like a pimple:
You grew on me
and swelled—
a sensation
I can no longer
ignore.

I tried to prick you away
but you left me
gaping
and in pain.
Just like a pimple.

PURPLE SCRUNCHIE

The first time
I used the five-peso
terry elastic
was on a humid
November day.
It should have been
chilly,
but no.
It was humid.

And singing rain
yet to spill
its costly droplets
on cracked brains
and unused recycled-paper notebooks
strewn haphazardly
throughout school.

To capture tendrils
of a bad-hair day
(yet again)
that sweep the particulates
from bitter-tasting

air:
the scrunchie left
my pulse
and took its beat away.

REGRESSION

Diverging paths
leading to somewhere
nowhere and everywhere
mud
and quashed
to rain-wet mush.

Singing voice
breaking through
falling and drenching
straggler
and lost
in the vat of destiny.

Striking bolt
tearing apart
into vestiges of what I was
once
and homeward
I plod on.

SMOKE

His name
is a word I could
not pronounce
nor spell.

All I do
is roll it around
my nicotine-stained
tongue
but never
say it or exhale
it like smoke.

Like, your being
kills me
with every breath.

SOLSTICE

the voice
of a Jack or Jill
echoes
like a song from elementary school
"bah bah black sheep…"
haunting
taunting

"have you any wool?"
none, except what's pulled
over my eyes
with their long standing myopia;
if only the wool
could double as a coat
to ward off
the chill of uncertainty

then again,
the (El Nino) heat
radiates
from my tuffet of safety
where to go
where to go (?)
I no longer know
the spider

I await
to keep me company

"twinkle, twinkle little star…"
things, I no longer wonder
what they are
all are just specks
of dust
in my high-powered vacuum cleaner

a solstice
of worlds that made me
now knitted
like frayed maroon yarn
of a friendship bracelet
I had worn through

a keepsake
enduring
as seasons
come and go

UGLY

a visage ripples crookedly

watch, as the looking glass
peels what is reflected
away

leaving a heart
never known to beat
in pulses
but in dreams left unrealized
to fester, unseen
to wilt away
in disconsolate bits of brown,
unremembered

thus, comes the time
to walk the thin dividing line
between you and yourself
and see nothing
through the endless masquerade

(you hate it —
much)

ULCER

Would you end
the stabbing pain?
Planted, plunged
deep into my gut:
a knife
that nothing wielded
no one held
but you.

WALLFLOWER

Bitterness embeds
itself
deep down.

And
I find myself
wishing
to see black-red
blood
stain your purity,
your hypocrisy.

You suck.

YELLOW-GREEN

I see the golden rays
glimmer
against my squinting eyes
against the Crocs-clad feet
that wear the pavement thin.

When, walking by,
with olive flesh
and a hundred hopes
and the murmur of second chances—

You look through my
sun-curtained visage
like it isn't there
scribbling dreams away
crookedly
picking the dried grass
to bits.

When you're now
the past
the fallen swipe of life:
you are the veined leaf
fluttering
in the summer wind.

WISPS OF MY SOUL

*Let your pain speak
Let the scar fade
After the crucible
Of silent shackles.*

AFAR

You are so far above
There is no road for me to take
To touch you, or reach for you
But I would leave all I have
For your sake

You are flawed and human
Yet they embrace all that you are
The way I would take you in my arms, too
But I never could
Because you are so far

I may never hold you close
You may never be mine
The way I want it to be
But my heart is yours
Until the end of time

From afar
I will look at you
From a distance
I will be there for you
From the shadows
I will give you all my love

If only I could have a moment
I would stop time
To be with you
If only I could live in dreams
Then I would fly to you

All these could never be
Yet I won't stop loving you

ARMS

Living in the stony silence of night
In the dark embrace of solitude
Listening to the echoes
In the empty halls of your heart–
Songs evil, lost, divine.

Through it all, though consumed,
Half-rotted by pride;
What your heart shall say
That I will abide.

I love you
Though you are still in pain
(from what had been)
How can I break through these walls
To hold you in my arms again?

AWAY

Remember my tears
They were shed for the loneliness
That I saw in your eyes
I tried to end the pain
But my own weakness wounds me

Remember my laughter
It rang because of hope
That each new day brings
I held on to the light
But darkness always comes

Remember my words
I write them for forever
I tried to make memories endure
But time washes away
These fleeting dreams made of sand

Remember my heart
It has always been yours
My love has never faded, only flourished
I tried to tell you
But I cannot always speak

I love you
Please remember this

BEGGING STREETS

Faceless, they contort
and silently scream
paper dolls
hanging on the clothesline
slapped
slapped about
by starched-white shirts
in virginal mockery.

A coin-regurgitated gumball:
cherry, chewed
staining
the betelnut-stained
pearly whites
flashed to starving
manual cameras running promises
ran dry.

Fluffy-gray air bubbles
from oily fire hydrants
give
the cleansing rain
in a summer spell,
as darker streams

wear down the asphalt gutter:
hence, not potable.

Falling, and struck
the can
wrenched
to its wounding gape;
inside,
the doughnut-like
copper coin
hears
the slightest plaintive cry
of thanks.

BLUE

Ending in a shattered
pot of clay:
no gold, yet the arch
(seven-tiered)
pours its sorrows
to overflowing.

Pattering on the
stained-glass edifice
of Saints, their halos
threatening to break
from the strain
of false reverence—
the shower
from heaven disbelieved.

Prisms falling
to cut against
cracked skin
with untrue tales
to tell.

When the gray tormented
shall clear away
doubtful Time alone knows;
the blue canvas, white-dotted,
my blinded eyes may
never behold.

DAMNATION

Every passing second
Is a hateful step closer
To an inescapable fate
Ever reminding
Of Time's irresistible power
Straight on to the very end

Every breath taken
Is made out of desperation
A final, futile bid for freedom
Ever hoping
That the air's purity would cleanse sins
Straight into immortality

Every drop of blood
Is hatefully alive
As it feeds the senses
Ever taunting
With lost chances and hopes
Straight into damnation

DANGER

Displayed at each turn, beckoning
So easy to get, easier to possess
Every single morsel bearing
The promise of an easy buy
Irresistible

Spread out before our eyes, dazzling
So good to the touch, better to the pocket
Every single piece bearing
The marks of far-off places
Undeniable

Underneath the surface, lurking
So dangerous, what we cannot see
Every shred bearing the risk
(of what it truly is)
The discarded and the unneeded
Expendable

DEBT

Everything ends
As the sun upon the day sets
As throbbing lives crumble to ashes,
And dust
When turmoil eventually quiets

Everything is ephemeral
As facets of light glint upon the clouds
As moments become now,
And nevermore
Leaving only traces on minds and souls

Everything is not ours
When debts forgotten are collected
When our lives,
In borrowed time
Become defined by what we owe

DECEPTION

Just don't listen to me
I lie
Time and time again
Until the falsehoods
Fall from my lips
As easily as breathing

Just don't say a word
I won't heed you
As always
You ask for nothing
You give everything
Without doubt

Just don't come any closer
I will push you away
With every moment
I am weaker
I am afraid
I can no longer hide

Just don't look at me
I can't bear the promise in your eyes
That you will fight for me
Without question
When asked to
But we are not just meant to be

Just walk away
Before I hold you back
Just leave
Before I run towards you
Just forget me
Before I learn to love you
Even more

Just stop

DELUSION

So steadfast and strong
This is how we believe
The powers and the promises to be
And so we become victims
Haplessly

So innocent and unhesitating
This is how we endure
The words and the creed written
And so we become pawns
Helplessly

So blind and ignorant
These we slowly turn out to be
As we fall into the trap of delusions
And so we become not the victor
Tragically

DEMOLITION

Spun all and sundry
In circles and whorls and loops
They took much
Out of nothing
That was already there.

There was hope
For tomorrow and warmth and bread
In the persevering form
Of desperately-constructed stalls
Rising from hot concrete.

Then heroes abound
In schemes and grandness and ambition
They bought desperation
With chunks of debris
Bringing an inevitable end.

DEPRIVATION

There is emptiness
Resting inside my heart
Sitting, waiting, reverberating
With cries

There is emptiness
Thrumming in countless stomachs
Malevolent, ruthless, unrelenting
Eating away

There is emptiness
Shedding darkness on souls innumerable
Plotting, unkind, misdirecting
I yearn to cast aside

DESPAIR

Believe me
When I tell you that
I see hope in your eyes
Believe me
When I tell you that
I see strength in your pain
And my salvation in your
carefully concealed despair

Believe me
When I look into your eyes
And say I see tears unshed
Believe me
When I try to touch your soul
But never could
And the cold simply
rips my heart apart

Believe me
When I say goodbye
In a halting whisper
Believe me
When I turn away
From your compelling madness

Believe me
That I am sorry
for being with you
That I love what I can
never have
That I walk away from you
before I no longer could

Believe me

DIFFERENCE

As heaven against earth
There are no roads to take
Oceans to sail across,
or rivers to conquer
To bridge the widening gap

As heaven against earth
The land could be so far away
Beyond understanding,
this vicious circle
Of the rise and fall of hopes

As heaven against earth
The golden stairway to the sky
Is but an illusion
a broken promise of salvation
At the end of a rainbow unseen

DISEASE

A smile full of promise
A smile so glinting
The knife-edge of
Lying lips
A kiss for silver pieces.

A dance in the dark
A dance upon knives
The *one-step, two-step* is a
Rhythmic soundtrack
Into honor's doom.

A seduction unrelenting
A seduction so ruthless
The ticks are
Your beautifully dressed, coiffed
Death-bringers.

DISTANCE

All alone
In the silence
Of endless thoughts
Poured into an empty page.

The distance: a wall of
Isles, rocks and foam
Travelled on by despair;
Breaking through.

As blood pools
On the scrunched forehead-skin,
The soul had long since
Been lamenting

Chipped away
By time and blindness.
In the other world
It yearned to see.

DISINTEGRATION

Cracking away
This is one powerful fate:
The land has succumbed to
Without a shred of resistance

Falling apart
This is what we have turned into:
The pawns of power-driven dreams
Divided and moved as they will us

Vanishing into nothingness
This is the true danger:
That threatens our people
We begin to lose our very selves

DIVINATION

See there?

So many visions and dreams
Countless, now formless, pathless
Made and cast out in fearsome ritual
Since time immemorial

See there?

So many souls treading on the roads
Countless, now aimless, hopeless
With minds hungry for enlightenment
Only to be disillusioned

See there?

So much smoke streaming all around
Impenetrable, ever bringing greyness
If only the mist will rise
Give way to light
So we could once more see.

There.

DUPLICATION

Times two

It might be our only chance
To have what we have so longed for
It might be the only time
To get what we have asked for
But could never otherwise own

Times two

Will they ever heed our side?
They only care for their statutes
Those broken countless times before
For us, it would seem,
These remain ironclad

Times two

There is but irony
In this bitter play of fortune
To take what we need
Away from our hands
Away from our reach

Times two

DUST

Drowning scratchy tones
screeched by a podium voice
that remains ever faceless:
subdued, a clacking staccato.

Rock-encrusted earth, weeded not for years,
chipped away in vain
by the dull-edged shovel;
crooked steel churning
visions acres wide.

In the purplish twilight glow
sparse through the sun-browned canopies,
a hunched soul
squints
as if grasping lost fragments
from hazy-gray auto exhausts.

Close to the lone theater's
cobbled threshold—
bidding two-bit thespians
(so-called)
Welcome.

Once the dustman;
a shrine of wrath and glory
long since crumbled
to bits.

He pounds
against the unrelenting soil
'til dusk
cloaks
a sleepy world.

DWELLING

Unyielding in your majesty
And proudly rising to the skies
You stand as silent witness
To conquest and pride

Incomparable in your mystique
And irresistible in your beauty
You are an honored paragon
Speaking of strength and freedom

Enduring in your virtue
And rich in your heart
You are the dwelling of dreams
Embodying hope
That could never be crushed

FALLEN FRAME

It's time to shut the door
and close it all away.
Since I've lost
what there is
to cry for.

It's time to put the razor blade
back on the shelf
(carefully, as not to nick
the fingertips with which I write)
and be like a clam:
tightly closed up.

Pry open with the tines,
if you dare,
when no one can.
No one can look
into this little world
and not be blinded.

It's time to pick up
the bits
of the picture frame
that found its way
off the peg.

But the photo's
left unscathed.

It's time to gather
the strewn odes
and flush them down the drain
and shout a slurred
"Nevermore!"
to an unheeding world.

As the fallen frame pieces,
thrown bit by bit
out of the window,
cut into hands
that had brushed away
silent salty rivers.

FOOD COURT

He sits
on the mocha-brown wood
and watches
the angst-ridden crowd
sweep by
like the dust
he used to sweep
when the back
still held.

(There is no end to them.)

He stays
unperturbed
in their midst
and hungers
for what he now cooks
(squid balls)
but can no longer afford
to sink
his (long gone) teeth
into.

He counts
in silent vigil
the cruel notes
of the cacophony
overwhelming
his time-ravaged senses.

He waits
for the minutes
of his half-hour work break
to pass
the way he waits
for the throng
to leave him
in its dusty wake.

JUXTAPOSITION

Soar high
in unbounded flight,
tread new-mown blades
with reverence.

'Tis the temple
of olden faith
borne witness
to glory and bloodshed.

With armaments splintered,
was carted away
to watch- and weep-
on the cruel stone stage.

RAINFALL

Witches' brew
enthralling stray spirits
that dare to savor
its citrus lure
Sumptuous
A prison of unseen walls.

Blessed water
soothing the sting of emptiness
that eats away
my life
Cool
An omen of redemption.

Fluid veil
deceiving eyes that pry,
that seek to see
my unilinear teardrops
Translucent
As the salty stream.

Acid wine
scorching like lust
that drunken poets fancy
in many a sonnet
Intoxicating
A being stripped of dreams.

SCARS IN SOLITUDE

Child, let your pain speak
let the scar fade
after the crucible
of silent shackles.

Leaves, aphid-white
drift there- and away;
a hope in balmy
rooms of soot.

Framed lovingly:
twisted images
of lost dreams
grasped in passing.

THE VOYAGE

Cutting through waves,
a swath of foam;
green-gray curdles
trail underfoot.

The raft of makeshift hopes
adrift for days —
and aimless —
steered blindly on.

Beyond the mist,
cobbles and rock-bits
make an inexorable testament
to lands beyond.

UNTOLD

You said that you were sorry
That you don't need me anymore
You said that you were leaving
And walked right out the door

How many times have you hurt me?
I truly have stopped counting
How many times have you left me?
Standing alone while it was raining

You said that all was wrong
That nothing works when we're together
You said we would only be lying
If we keep talking of forever

So go on, tell me
Whatever you want to say
Go on, be true
There seems to be no other way

Tell me I'm not the ideal
I know all your reasons why
Tell me I'll never be strong
That I'm always lacking in your eyes

Tell me everything that hurts
This forever hopeful heart of mine
Tell me how to make you stay
Just don't tell me goodbye

DROPS OF MY BLOOD

Alone once more, I face
The beginning.
Alone once more, I know
There really is no end.

A FAT GIRL THING

hanging over
a hunk of ham, of flesh
a slice of the delicatessen
in my fever dreams

slices, and chunks
ripples of sinfully sweet
saccharine and corn
dripping and my senses
peak
(unbearably)

I but pinch my sides
bruised by the too-tight denims
that cut between the cheeks of my
meandering butt

it always hurts like hell
again, and again

as I look at the emaciated
hoochie mamas
with their belly-tanks,
their platform shoes that do not crack
from the burden,
the silver crosses caressing their
firm (upright) bosoms

my hands find the draping tips
hanging over a rolling middle
to squeeze, and squeeze

AIMLESS

Shall I wait for you?
I scorn and shun
The moments when you are not by my side
You wander aimlessly
Reticent and seeking

Shall I look into your eyes?
I fear and dread
The time when I could no longer lie
I pretend uselessly
My will is futile and bent

Shall I touch you?
I do not wish to
Because the moment I do
You will know the truth
That I hide

Shall I speak to you?
My words come listlessly
Hiding my true yearning
I shall say
The things I do not mean

Shall I love you?
My heart could never lie
Even if forever I persist
To deceive it, and deny
That it has long since belonged to you

I have to try

ANCHOR

Call for my passion
Heedless as I am
Reckless and unstoppable
I shall hear you

Sadness and hate
May consume me
But never
Shall I turn away
From you

Speak to my soul
As I wait for hope
Being the child
That I always will be
Love shall be my anchor
In this stormy sea
Lighting my path of uncertainty
As forever
I believe it shall endure
Give your heart
To me

ARDOR

I wish that we may be together
In a way that we fear nothing
And believe in everything
That we have

I wish that we may be stronger
In a way that we do not hold back tears
But cry freely to let the pain out
So what's left inside is happiness
And hope, perhaps

I wish that we may love as purely
As the spring rushes over the rocks
That the years will wear our bodies away
But our hearts never stop flowing
Towards eternity

BACK IN THE FOOD COURT

The primary-hued neon tubes
make a lurid flashing cacophony—
silently beckoning.
As throngs of weary hearts file by
too careworn to care, or
surreptitiously glance.

In cold mechanical precision
roams the legion
of tightly-clothed brawny
busboys:
Taking the unwanted away,
those abandoned
garish-orange trays.

In this room
where the air is tepid,
and spruced
with the distant memory
of onions
and soda gone flat—
there echo

footfalls of tales unbounded
by number.

But all
just come to pass
in that stream.

BLACK CAT

Sign of the cross.

It's a phase like everybody else's:
A bit of futile struggles here (I annotate),
sneezy tears there.
Desire is a lollipop I lick at
and spit its taste away.
Only to visit confession
by cutting class.

Don't forget
the dawn rendezvous
of hazy brown-and-white cylindrical pilings
caressing my breath,
of bitter foam kissing
my burning lips,
of heat cascading
down my neck and throat
and chest
and belly.

The water runs over me, to waken.

But then, I always seek
and find
and feel.

BLOOD

Thank you.
For the pain
through which I grope my way
in dazed wakefulness.
The void, where
my tongue-tips
catch the essence
of a hungering moon.

Thank you.
For the mead-like meat
of thoughts
long struck by paradox.
Scratching away.
Clawing, until the coagulating life
ensues to stream.
Wanderlust, and more.

Thank you.
For the flesh,
bathed in endless moaning
trembles.
Lined with pain
from endless moaning
trembles.

For the flesh,
seeking the uneven
tease.

Thank you.
For the constancy.
The mundane.
This strange little
taste that leaves
a parched throat half-open.
In expectation.

DARK

I hope you will see
Right through the blankness
That is my countenance
It is not emptiness
But a mask of pain

I hope you will hear
Right through the quiet
That is my outward self
It is not silence
But a rage no one will understand
Hence I keep

I hope you will feel
The beating of my heart
That no one knows is still there
I am not stone
Nor darkness, nor torment
I am shadow
Wanting light
I am my unknown self
Needing you

DAUNTLESS

I stare into darkness
Wary, watching
Ever so calculating
And cold to the watchful eye

I speak to no one
With nothing to impart
But the blank slate that is my soul
That some say
Isn't there anymore

I hear nothing
Not their taunts
Or wishes for my supposed absolution
I am stone, strong, steadfast
Proud, invincible

I am unmoving
In the rain of time
In the thunder of pain
I am waiting for you
To let me feel again
Breathe again
Live again

DAWN

Eventide slowly falls
Under the stars
That blink and fool
Night becomes my shelter
In this cheerless solitude
Call to me
With your song
Ever promising

Dawn slowly rises
Over my wanting heart
Another waiting chance
For my redemption
Another life
Of nothing and everything
Time flows me by
Ever taunting

Present slowly comes
Enfolding and unfolding
Dawn and dusk
In a circle never-ending
Rising and falling
Eternally, so shall I go
Onwards and seeing

DEATH

I know you—
a face among persevering faces
I have been told your story
countless times before
but salvation comes too late, each time

I heard you—
a voice among countless others
and the loud drumbeat
of a heart long since waiting
for Fate's kinder hand

Now
I wonder how it felt
for you to feel
the tearing of bullets
into your body and soul,
as the metal shrieked
and rent your dreams asunder.

DEFIANCE

I toil against the sun
As it beats down on me
In an evil haze of drought
Drying the sparse well of hope

I toil against the storm
As it roars all around me
In a vengeful carnage
Bringing death to dreams

I toil against desolation
As its hook cuts into my heart
In irresistible fatality
Denying the bounty of life

DELIVERANCE

Away from the entrapment
Of their deceitful shrouds
And prettified lies
It was my time to live
This tribulation is my emergence

Away from being broken
By their enduring falsehoods
And stolen power
It was my time to rise
This tribulation is my odyssey

Away from being destroyed
By the hidden anarchy of old paths
And all-consuming greed
It was my time to strike
This tribulation is my redemption

DEPTHS

You have nothing, you say
Nothing to fight for
No reason to live or die
No battle, nor twisted reasons to lie
Just an empty heart beating
Deep into the moonless night

You have everything, you say
Everything to hate and shun
Pained endlessly
In the merciless light of the sun
All the countless whispers
Of judgment and persecution
Everything to carry, burdened evermore
Deep into your loneliness

You have me, you say
I to fight against, or madly hate
To die with, perhaps
To share your pain
In the harsh embrace of a cruel life
I gather the fragments
Of a heart long since unfound
And try so hard
To make you whole once more

And I have you, I say
To hold on to, to madly love
To live with—forever, perhaps
Or maybe beyond

In this unyielding existence
We shall find ourselves once more
So give me your heart
And we'll have our love to fight for

DESIRE

I feel my heart steaming towards you
I am wrought with the flames
Of passion
Consuming me
Until I am nothing more
Than smoldering ash

I feel my body steaming towards you
I am drawn without resistance
To your fiery seduction
Burning deep into me
Until I am nothing more
Than trembling desire

I feel my mind steaming towards you
I am controlled by this irresistible fascination
And unrelenting obsession
Taking over me
Until I am nothing more
Than sheer madness

I feel my soul steaming towards you
I shall sweetly surrender
All that I have
And all that make me
Until I am nothing more
Than your wasted possession

DESTINATION

Traverse the ocean
Let my voice swim
Through the rippling waves
Glittering
Beneath the golden sun

Traverse the sky
Let my heart soar
In the sheltering clouds
Embracing
My memories of home

Traverse the miles
That I may be there
Where I am most needed
Choosing
The road of tomorrow

DISCORD

just like a razor
and its cutting edge
voices and gazes of dissent
slash through my flesh
but never draw blood

the cacophony of lies
from all around
strike greater than a killing blow
I painfully am close by
insurmountable I remain

the festival of unadulterated ugliness
and the breakdown it brings
forces and persists against
my indomitable will
unheeding I remain

DISRUPTION

i. **Lost**

Brainfreeze
is all there is to it.
Nothingness
in my line of vision.

ii. **Taken**

You live in my head
Like cancer
You disrupt my system
As a virus would
A system embracing doom
In unguarded naiveté

You live in my head
Like a dream
You make me waken
In the dead of night
Breathless, empty, wanting
In the unforgiving dark

You live in my head
Like an echo
You speak without yielding

As the unwelcome does
An unwanted temptation
Taking me by storm

iii. Sightings

I am blind
I cannot see behind the mask
I pull over my own eyes
Like a curtain
My mask
My disguise

I am blind
I am bound
By my own darkness
My own unforgiving soul
My own expectations
My pride

I am blind
And I am safe
In this void
Where I remain
Untouched
Untouchable

DIVERGENCE

Here I am
At the crossroads
Of thought and memory and sensation
Awaiting the curtains to rise.

The ink
In the pen
Of unbridled spirit
Speak and question and speak
some more.

So unveiling
In brutal honesty
The halves and shadows along the way
That none may fall prey.

DIVIDE

I see the world
in a flood of dusty light-bulbs—
A vision pained by Time's merciless inquest
Into a haggard soul;
But I plod onward.

Beneath a skylight
that threatens to cave in,
I bow my head in silent supplication
And my dreams scuttle away
Into the pages of a worn,
forgotten book.

I became a servant:
Hoping, waiting in vain
Until I am but a vegetable
Swimming in a lake of sweat and depravity.

But the dust, too, shall tire and fall
And I will find the light
Streaming—first in puddles,
then in waves—
into my path.

Alone once more, I face
The beginning.
Alone once more, I know
There really is no end.

DREAMS

It is now time to see
Right through the turmoil
Running its course through our lives
And way beyond

It is now time to break free
Right through the ice
Locking us into a standstill
Forever buried beneath past sins

It is now time to wake up
Bring dreams to life and share a vision
Of our legacy unburdened and unchained
From transgressions past

DRIBBLE

I. Dribbling, dribbling
against the hardcourt
of your upper-lip stubble
in dark brown streaks
and streaky white.

II. Rivulets of hot fudge
sundae toppings
dispensed as
circular tracks or soot-stained snowflakes
into fragile plastic cups
taking the generous swell of
a beer belly.

III. Or my own
rounded stomach
(I so desperately try to conceal)
with the three-month life
you had spilled
into it.

IV. The way your choco fixes
lose themselves
to your voracious
appetite.
And greed.

DRIFT

Make me see
All that I have to understand
So the raging inside can quiet.
In soothing tones
Hum a lullaby for me
Make the tears dry away
Into forgetfulness.

Seeking shelter–
Underneath its canopy
I could sing one last song of love;
Onward I will journey
Never to live
Back in the past.

FLIGHT

It's just like a rocket.
I arrive to the careen
of ceramics, an artful juggling
with an unfeeling wall.
And dodge.

The new haircut
left unnoticed, now adorned
with glass bits from jalousies,
beer mugs that always reek,
and glasses that leave stains
on woodwork.

It's just like a home-run hit.
I enter to the incoming rush
of a thirty-peso spatula
and deftly make the catch.

The uniform, rust-stained,
had eaten heartily ahead.
Splotches of tonight's
savory viand, plus the neighbor's
complimentary birthday leche flan.

Thus, I contemplate
a career in sports.

HOLY WAR

i.   reckoning
has come
my mama tells me
that I am a heretic
that I'd rather wear
my unwashed denim cut-offs
than kiss the feet
of elevated saints

ii.   Sunday morn
is a struggle
when I'd rather keep my eyes
closed
and chat to a campy dream-
    conscription
lamenting
in Freudian skerries
than dress in white
stained twice too many
by unexpected flows
'neath the pulpit

iii. a ratty blanket
     too dirty to be washed
     is a shield
     of futility against salvation
     (it ain't free, no)
     that sells itself
     by stealing slumber and cuckoo projections
        and Chinese soap operas
        right before teen show reruns

iv. endlessly
     I search for weapons
     but there is no fighting
     a blast
     of the cold shower
     or the threat of cutting off my
     fiat sustenance

v.   the beads I gather

vi. and I head for the final stop
     glossed lips moving
     in silent feverish whispers
     of supplication

SILENCE

living under the tearstained sky
left all alone and staring
way up high
at the gray
or whatever color in my way

I saw nothing
but the blinding dusk
I felt nothing but your touch
burning my life away
in memory you killed me

with one look
nothing matters but the pain
that I want from your caress
and you never say a word
to make me
catch my breath again

go away to the songs that you sing
to the crash of glass
as the shrapnel cuts into you
I hope you bleed
I hope your life spills
like the milk
that I cry over

SMOKE 2

I take a toke
of your purity
and realize
the sweetness
exploding within me.

Injecting life
like the amphetamine
in my morning espresso
or the cheap instant
or whatever
coffee in my cup.

The scent filling
my being—
that heady scent
is your frankincense
kiss.

ABOUT THE AUTHOR

Shirley Siaton writes edgy and evocative poems and stories. Her worlds are in a deliciously dark cross-section of the romance, neo-noir, action, fantasy, new adult, and contemporary genres.

She has several books of poetry and fiction released since February 2023. Her first book is the free verse collection *'Black Cat and other poems.'* She also pens juvenile literature as Shirley Parabia.

She is an award-winning writer, poet and journalist in English, Filipino and Hiligaynon, lauded by the Stevan Javellana Foundation, Philippine Information Agency, and West Visayas State University. Her essays, short stories and poems have been published internationally in print and digital media. Her multi-lingual plays have been staged in the Philippines.

Shirley is a black belt in Shotokan Karate and an international certified fitness coach. Originally from Iloilo City, she is based in the Middle East with her husband and two daughters.

ON THE WEB

Shirley's official website:
shirleysiaton.com

Complete reading guide:
shirley.pub

Subscribe to Shirley's VIP list for free exclusive updates:
newsletter.shirleysiaton.com

www.ingramcontent.com/pod-product-compliance
Lightning Source LLC
LaVergne TN
LVHW040057080526
838202LV00045B/3675

*9 7 8 6 2 1 4 9 0 0 9 8 5 *